Sojourn Into The Night

Sojourn Into The Night

A MEMOIR OF THE PERUVIAN RAINFOREST

Elaine Donadio

http://ElaineDonadioWrites.wordpress.com
elainewrites@earthlink.net

ISBN: 1532979711
ISBN 13: 9781532979712
Library of Congress Control Number: 2016907108
CreateSpace Independent Publishing Platform
North Charleston, South Carolina

Acknowledgements

With special thanks to Marti Dobkins - MarJim books (iformat4u@aol.com)
for formatting this book.

With special thanks to Judy Bullard (customebookcovers@cox.net) for help
with the cover design.

Dedication

This book is dedicated to Andrea and Matthew with love

A tattered cloak of ebony
backlit
by the stars
and the full March moon.
Unveiled,
the tributary of the mighty
Amazon,
river of the Napo people,
still,
but for the shatter
of the small boat
quietly coursing ahead,
never suggesting the abundance of
life
concealed beneath its depths.

Exalted forest fashions shadows,
at this moment in time,
occasioned by flashlights.
At eye level,
buttress roots spread wide,
staunch soldiers
earnest in their mission.

Lianas reach up
with wooden fingers
in communion with arboreal giants.

Whispers echo
as we struggle
to keep our presence
unperceived by the creatures
hidden amidst
the luxuriant foliage,
as we endeavor to
camouflage ourselves,
as well,
lest our facades
be cracked open
to reveal truths
we prefer to keep hidden
and our social behaviors
give us away.

"Shhh," the guide warns
as his five passengers
break the rule of silence.
Gregarious by nature,
we must learn
to blend
with our surroundings
in our unfamiliar roles
as learners,
observing rules
not of our making.

A discordant choir.
Warble, trill, chirp.
Each creature with its own tune.
Buzz, hum, croak, squeak.
Droning, drumming repetitions
of unharmonious cries
throughout the night.
Yet, our speech
interrupts their rhythm.

Under cover of darkness
we slink through
the great biome.
Searching
the patterns of the sky,
the upside down view
of Orion
serves as a bookmark.
The Southern Cross
comes into view,
then the Centaur,
seemingly magnified
from this opaque vantage point,
unique in their placement
in the southern hemisphere,
now revealing themselves
to the visitors
from the continent to the north
on a quest for knowledge
and enlightenment.

"Whuh, whuh, whuh,"
the gentle flapping
wings of the
Amazonian bat
disturbed by the beams of light,
spied only for an instant.
Too close for comfort,
three gliding mammals
flit overhead
in succession
before seeking shelter
among the countless leaves
of the rainforest.

Bats

Live in social groups.

World's only flying mammal.

Echolocate prey

by sending out clicking sounds.

Furry bodies with webbed wings.

"Stop," the guide
murmurs to the boat captain.
A single beam
highlights a solitary figure
embracing the tip of a leaf.
Perhaps the katydid
did not fear us,
or perhaps
its instincts told it to remain,
playing the odds
that we did not see it,
as green as the leaves surrounding it
and just as still.

Katydid

Prolonged antennae,
Green, camouflaged bush cricket
Chirps evening song.
Egg-nymph-adult, live one year.
Protein source for birds, bats, monkeys.

Moving on,
flashlights zigzag,
then circle,
searching
the obscure forest
for signs of life.
"Croak, croak, croak."
Steering the boat in the direction
of the guttural warning,
eyes adjusting,
with spotlights
on the lone bullfrog
bellowing
on a leftover tree stump,
a private island in the midst
of a liquid world.

Our boat captain
gingerly pulls the boat
alongside the bullfrog's territory
while our guide
deftly grabs the bloated amphibian
and holds him firmly with two
hands.
Not at all appreciating the specter of
cameras flashing
as we admire his features,
the bullfrog uses his powerful legs to hop
onto my lap as I watch the scene
with wide-eyed curiosity.

"Get it off me!"
I try to escape but there is no place to go
on this tiny boat filled to capacity.
The more I yell,
The more the bullfrog holds his ground.
"Croak, croak, croak."
Bellowing back in what becomes
a war of sounds,
one frightened, one assertive,
the bullfrog stares right at me
loudly communicating his displeasure
at being abruptly snatched
from the comfort
and safety of his home.

The guide scoops up the bullfrog,
holding it tightly until he can return it
to its just place.
"Sorry for the drama,"
the guide apologizes
to the bullfrog
who continues to complain long after
we leave his little kingdom.

Bullfrog

Alien species.

Voracious, will eat friends, too.

Permeable skin thus,

canary in the cage.

Nocturnal amphibian.

Flashes of red, orange, pink
interrupt
the monotonous
achromatic backdrop—
bromeliads, orchids and lilies,
familiar sights in an unfamiliar
waterscape.
We come to a small cluster of trees
when the guide whispers, "Go back."

Putting the boat in reverse,
the captain awaits further instructions.
"…to the right."
Smiling to himself,
the guide shares his
accomplishment.
Focusing flashlights,
the image of a walking stick
slowly emerges from the overlapping leaves.
Almost undistinguishable from brown,
dried up wood,
the insect remains immobile,
about twelve inches long,
not making a move,
not making a sound.

Walking Stick

Looks like sticks or twigs.

Adapts to fool predators.

Sways to walk; eats plants.

Food for birds, reptiles, spiders.

Most vulnerable to bats.

Gentle tickling sensations
on my sandaled feet
can only mean one thing.
I don't see anything.
I don't hear anything.
Virtually undetectable,
but dangerous, nevertheless.
Mindful
of my yellow fever vaccine.
Thankful
for my malaria pills.
Regretful
of my carelessness.
Forgetful
in changing back
into sneakers and high socks
pulled over my pants legs.

I imagine
the angry welts
that will manifest themselves
by morning,
and I begin to itch.
Grabbing my insect repellent
from my backpack,
I spray it on my feet, limbs and hair,
pat it on my face,
and for good measure,
saturate my clothing.

Aware that I am overreacting,
my companions laugh
at my frantic efforts
to counteract
the bites
from the mosquitoes
of the rainforest.

"I'm not done yet."
I laugh when I realize
that I am a comical sight.
"Now for the dragon's blood!"
I massage drops of dark, red liquid
known as "sangre de grado,"
purchased earlier that day
from a shaman
in ceremonial headdress and beads,
into each throbbing red circle,
rubbing in a circular motion
until it turns a milky white.
The remedy works quickly.
The itch and the swelling begin to recede.

All is quiet
again
as we continue
on our journey.

"Shhh."
Directed by the
beams of light,
our eyes adjust,
revealing a butterfly
unique
to these environs.

Its wings are open now.
Two staring "eyespots"
give the impression
of an owl's face.
In shades of brown,
its form
slowly emerges
from the tree trunk
of the same color.

We don't dare to move.
The creature flutters its wings,
then closes them
as it alights on a single leaf,
allowing us to admire it
in proud profile.

Owl Butterfly

Wings collect sun rays
To act as solar heaters.
Fly at dusk and dawn.
Safer with its owl-like mask,
Still, prey for bats, birds, frogs, snakes

Hearing the unheard.
Seeing the unseen.
Sensing the invisible.
The imperceptible delineation of an object
amid its cover,
truly camouflaged
but for the keen eye
of the rainforest guide
with an extraordinary power
of night vision,
fluently communicating
in a language not his own.

With awe and respect,
perceiving his world
through his senses.
A steadfast scout in a wilderness
unknown to me
but understood in its entirety by this great teacher
who stands before me
appearing as an ordinary human,
but with depths of knowledge
and intuition that surpass my own.

Seeing the world through
another's lens,
I know my limitations
in a way never before revealed.

Unescorted,
I would have feared the night,
lost in a maze
of ambiguous paths
leading to
unwished for places.
Confused
by the cacophony of
undefined sounds,
I would have seen nothing,
even that
in plain sight.

I vow this night
to soften my edges,
to allow myself
to evolve
like
a metamorphosed butterfly
into
a sentient being
willing
to look past
what appears to be,
now inclined
to see
what is.